# ratified

# ratified

*Virginia warbey*

*The Merdon Marque*

First published by *The Merdon Marque* 2004

Photograph by kind permission of Joyce Warbey

Cover artwork courtesy of Kathleen Bryson:

Northern Lights:
*Snows Older Than History*

Published and typeset in Great Britain in 2004

by

*The Merdon Marque*
11 Swanton Gardens, Chandler's Ford
Hampshire SO53 1TP

Printed in Great Britain by
Sarsen Press, Winchester, Hampshire

ISBN 1 872340 17 2

# Virginia Warbey, 1968-2004

Virginia was killed in a car crash on June 10th, 2004. It was a Thursday night, at the time when the writers' group she belonged to, Chandler's Ford Writers, was meeting as we do each week to discuss our work, to support and help each other. Virginia was a member of the group from 1994 onwards – she even wrote a poem about how much the group meant to her ('better than sex, almost.')

Virginia was born and raised near Rainham in Essex. Her first writing success won her a Doctor Who novel, but undeterred, she continued producing poetry and prose and went on to study English at Liverpool University and an MA in Creative Writing from Chichester. She earned her living as a librarian, but her real job was her writing. Two of her novels – *The Ropemaker's Daughter and The Carradine Diary* – were published by Diva under her married name of Virginia Smith. At the time of her death she was living with her much loved partner, Lisa Wing, and was enjoying being step-mum to Lisa's three children. Virginia was also hard at work on her new novel, and talking of putting a second poetry collection together.

When someone dies tragically, suddenly and young, it's easy to see it as a life cut in half, to think of things not done. But what Virginia did do in her life – the loving partnerships and friendships she established, the poetry and prose she completed, the happy memories she left behind – are a very special kind of legacy. The first poetry collection Virginia had published, when she was just 22, is called *A Legacy of Echoes*, but the poems included in *Ratified* aren't echoey, reflected voices. They are strong and clear, and uniquely hers. Virginia's sense of humour, emotional honesty, love of animals, of sex, words, friends – these are all here. Perhaps, as the American poet Billy Collins says, poetry is written as a way of cheating on death, of leaving something of ourselves that outlasts our own lives.

As writers and friends of Virginia, we wanted to make sure her work was not lost or forgotten but enjoyed, just as everyone who knew Virginia herself will not forget her or her ability to bring happiness to the gloomiest day.

Chandler's Ford Writers
September, 2004

## Acknowledgements

The publishers would like to acknowledge the editors of the following publications in which some of these poems first appeared:

Orbis; Poetry Life; Staple; Acumen; Envoi; New Forest Poetry Society Anthologies 1996, 1997 &1998; Mslexia.


*A Dream of Falling* won fourth prize in the 1996 Tandem Poetry Competition.

*Poppies* won first prize in the 1996 Hastings Poetry Competition.

*Greyhound at Hallelujah Bay* won fourth prize in the 1996 Poetry Life Competition.

*Cedarwood* won first prize in the 1997 Retort Poetry Competition.

*You* won first prize in the 1997 Chiltern Poetry Competition.

*Abishag* was runner-up in the 1997 Northwords Poetry Competition.

*Magdalen* won first prize in the 1998 Hastings Poetry Competition.

*Falling in Love with the Lion* won first prize in the 1998 Poetry Life Competition.

*Drunk* won second prize in the 1998 Petra Kenney Poetry Competition.

*Ratified* was runner-up in the 1998 New Forest Poetry Society Competition.

*Sex Like Dancing* won third prize in the 1998 Barnet Poetry Competition

*Spitfire* won third prize in the 2000 Wells Poetry Competition.

*The Wedding at Cana* was commended in the 2000 Hastings Poetry Competition.


Chandler's Ford Writers apologise for any omissions to the list above.


They gratefully acknowledge Lisa Wing's input and permission. *Making a Difference* is included for her.

# Contents

## Crayola Love

It isn't the sex so much,
the way our bodies seem
to mesh together -
arc pleasure
simultaneously,
breathing falling into
rhythm like hands
beating distant drums.

No, it isn't the sex so much.
Instead it is the way
your soul, like a crayon
left too long in the sun,
melts slowly
into mine; fiery reds
and oranges
infuse ice blue, until
the you and I become
a canvas of us.

Passion cools -
indelible colour remains.

## The Joys of Amphibious Living

It would be about having somewhere to go,
when the earth grew too solid, too certain;
finding something soft as love,
green as the beginnings of a lie; a new substance –
liquid, twilight, shady places.

We'd receive the world through our skin,
pressing our stomachs against moist surfaces
and taking in the sweetness that way,
without having to think about it or give anything
    back in return.
Sticky pads on our hands and our feet would
cling to the angles of buildings,
the steep sides of streets.
When conversation flagged,
we'd simply excuse ourselves, slip away,
sleep upside down on each other's ceilings.
Little gills would grow like buttercups
behind our ears, our breath a smoky foliage
filled with quiet.

Water is denser than air.
We wouldn't hurry even if we wanted to.
We'd have to take our time, give ourselves up
    to the flow;
swallowing seeds of sunlight,
feeling only how the current touches and moves.

The North American Leopard Frog
is no bigger than your thumb, but he has muscles
of elastic, so strong that they can leap him
        clear of waterfalls.
He flies to dry land.
Perhaps that's all it takes then, that resolve,
believing it possible to exchange one element
        for another,
believing that belief is enough.

## Cedarwood

Cedarwood, a smooth plane smelling of sunlight,
water, the soft heat of fingertips.

I watch you through the window as I work.
I watch you at the well and in your father's house.
You stoop down and your blue skirts crumple against your skin,
sticking to your thighs in the fly-blown heat.
You lift yourself carefully these days.

The cedarwood grows warm beneath
my hands, begins to darken.

I watch you as I work, and it's as if I do not know you;
you with your secrets, with your blue skirts
crumpling and the screen of your lashes low.
Did you look like this for him, Mary?
When his hands melted against you,
was this the smile that opened up
and called him home?
Another man's child sleeps in you,
another man's love like a splinter, a stone.
Some days, I cannot bear to look at you.

The cedarwood burns red and gold at night.
When the blade catches and slices, sparks
of colour fill the room. Shadows
loom and fall.

You will come into my house, Mary, sit at my table
with your stone jars and the wedding blankets
your sisters have made,
and my heart will bloom clear through my clothes;
a love gift, in spite of it all.
Sometimes, the wood chooses its own form.

I will take you, forgive you,
but who knows if my skies will fall
and the desert dust claim me,
the day your son turns and I see in his face
who his father is.

## Drunk

At first, it's just a taste,
a glimmer on the tongue;
a discernible warmth that makes you
lift your chin as you swallow.
Then a gesture behind your breastbone,
an agitation of hands, a bird in a cage with the door
set open, and a sky.

An ascendancy now, a smile that won't go away.
This is the best part by far.
With a trickle of gold in your veins and that astonishing
ascendancy, everything is possible.
You want to scrawl out the truth in your blood,
share the secret,
open up your body like a ripe watermelon
and let whoever comes feast on your flesh.
You want everyone to taste the sweet core of you,
the suddenly sweet core of you.

The tide takes you, lifts your limbs into the air
as if you are dancing,
and words spill into your mouth and out again, clever as sin,
sharp as the teeth of this thing
in your glass.

It's love now, of course it's love,
and your eyes narrow, take the measure of everything.
You are a guru.
People will come to you for wisdom, enlightenment.
There is no question you cannot answer.
Just the sound of your voice will heal,
the touch of your fingers,
the warm heart of your sex.
You will fuck the world to sleep and still have
the strength to move mountains.

Drunk, you are a hero.
You are loved,
and tomorrow's trail of blood,
tomorrow's rituals of sleep and censure
are nothing compared to this.
You always knew the shape that
God would take.
See? You can lift him to your mouth.
You can swallow him.

## In Love With John Boy Walton

Creamed corn. Chicken stew.
A meat-loaf fresh from the stove.
I taste the warm and let it linger, slow-time,
as if this is where I belong.

I've always thought it; mountains that bear my name,
those winding streams like threads of coloured
wool against the green.
I could gather them up, ask Grandma how to crochet.
I know she'd know. We could patchwork a cover for John Boy's bed,
something for the cold that shivers in and makes
the pencil tremble in his fingers as he writes.
I see him through the glass,
his blond hair falling forward,
his breath a bubble filled with unassuming air.
He'd take me to the top of Walton's Mountain if I asked,
sweet with the smell of applewood and aspen,
the honey-bee hum of his voice.
We'd gather juniper berries,
pale green needles from beneath the trees.
He'd ask if he could kiss me.
I'd say yes.

Later, in the heart of the white-washed house,
Grandpa would teach me a hot-shoe shuffle
while the others looked on, beaming,
and when they called to each other goodnight,
my name would be there too.

In the morning, I'd sit at the breakfast table,
innocent as a bud, humming with possibilities.
I'd leave my old self behind, begin anew,
but not before I'd taken John Boy up onto the mountain
and done what I've always wanted to do;
whipped off his glasses, his blue dungarees,
taught him a thing or two.

## Essex Sheep

End of the motorway, rush hour Friday,
and there they are;
black-nosing through the fence,
breathing in the fumey air as if it tastes
of lakeland green, mountain clover.

Not like other sheep,
not trembling in the twilight, or huddled
underneath a tree until the noise is over.
No. Instead, they're plump on traffic sounds.
Their wool is shining grey with brawl and bustle.
Like rugby players shouldering a scrum they stand
and bare their topaz teeth;
these sons of Romford,
Essex born
and bred on grass as dry as fear.

I watch them as I pass, wind down my window,
listen for the murmur of their
woolly gangster talk,
and they acknowledge me; Essex girl come home,
remembering a day when I was little;
Kenny Browning's Irish cousin, over
for the summer, saying he would beat me up
behind the refuse tip -

how he came toward me, soft fists
raised, his eyes watery,
pale blue as the skies of Donegal.
And all I did was breathe a puff of Essex
in his face.
He turned and ran away.
Sometimes, even now, that's all it takes.

Essex sheep.
I greet my own reflection in the mirror,
catch a gangster glint of topaz teeth.

## A Nest of Bones

Planting spring onions in my mother's back yard,
I uncover a nest of bones; stirrup and anvil small,
a tinkling together of tiny bones, poking up
through the ravelled dirt, vertical, grey-white like the sky,
and I recall the day we put them there,
remember sobbing on the doorstep that it wasn't my fault,
even though I knew it was.
I'd left the cage door open so the budgie
had escaped, flown straight for the window,
head down, intent on the colour of bright,
sensing freedom, branches, green-gold feathered air.

Now I roll his bones like matchsticks in my palm,
weightless, curving away from my grasp and the old grasp of earth.
I wait for them to gather, reconstitute, fly away.

They say that at the battle of Verdun,
hundreds of men were buried alive in the mud.
They died where they stood, bayonets fixed.
If you go there, even now, you'll still see
the tips of the blades, grey-white like the sky,
poking up through the ravelled dirt; a nest of bones beneath,
a tinkling together of tiny bones intent on the colour of bright.
I wait for them to gather, reconstitute, fly away.

# Find Summore

My two year old godson thinks that blackberries
are called *find summore*.
Weekends at the country park,
where blackberry bushes
crowd in a cloud of bruise and blue,
his parents point for him and smile.
'Find some more, Joshua,' they say,
'find some more',
and he tangles his tiny footsteps with blackberry roots,
fills his tupperware pot to the top
with what he thinks are *find summore*.

At the supermarket, his eyes grow wide
when the trolley he is parked in, pauses
at the fruit counter.
'Buy some *find summore*,' he insists,
reaching his fists for blackberries,
taking language onto his tongue
like the sweet tang of fruit.

Let this last for a while, I ask.
Let language not come
to confound him with its confines.
Let him be free to order his world to taste
the same as he thinks.
He'll soon learn.

## Greyhound at Hallelujah Bay

At Hallelujah Bay I watched you fishing,
thin rod bouncing light and low, the sun a glare
of yellow on your knuckles clenching tight,
unfolding, again tensing; as if a sea of bass or bubbled mullet
were paddling home to how your fingers moved and curled.
I sat a little way behind and waited, hugged my knees in tight
and thought a miracle to soothe you; dreamed you Galilean buckets full,
ourselves a tiny fire in the twilight,
fish-smoke,
little bones of wrinkled wood charred white...
Still nothing.

I left you fishing, waded backward from the shore,
the pebble line, the gravel sound of marbles in a bag,
and in the dunes I found a greyhound sleeping, a greyhound body
stretching long and breathing deep as if the sea were rumbling soft
inside his nubbled ribcage. Black, grey at the edges,
his long nose specked with flecks of hair as white as milk,
a snout fresh out
of the cat's bowl, his eyelashes thick as a girl's.
I watched his eyelids flicker, watched
his muscles tense, then suddenly a voice far off
was calling; Jet... *Here boy. Come on Jet...*
and he was wide awake and up,
the traps were open, hare set free, his body
lithe and long and gracious in the rushing green,
attending to the blood-run of his training.
He was gone before I knew
he'd ever really been.

At Hallelujah Bay I watched you fishing,
tried not to hear the noise of traps, the summer
crowds, tried not to see a blur of hare rush by me.
I hugged my knees in tight and watched and
made the scent of fish-smoke
my forgetting, but when at last you doubled back and turned your
thin rod spinning, my heart ran cold, and free,
to see
that all you'd caught was sea weed
dark as blood.

## Hebrew Moon

Came home today with pockets full of shells;
Dog Winkles, Blue-Rayed Limpets, Slender Colus',
Ox-Heart Clams - all clicking small maracas,
familiar shapes, accustomed shapes,
their sea-worn grooves like Braille beneath my hands.

I'd knelt to melt the shingle with my touch,
all morning searching pebbles for the unexpected
edge
of something new,
and then I found it; Hebrew Moon -
all the way from the Aegean,
its creamy whorls, a tale of tides and sunlight,
its columella like porcelain,
as flawless as a thing shed from the sky;
a bubble of ice,
its blue eye startled by dry land.

I polished it clean, hurried it home in the agitated
palm of my hand, not believing.
All the way from the Aegean for me to find,
solid as a word said many times,
and yet
dissolving.

Long before I reached my door,
my pockets grew unbearable with shells;
loud with the sound of familiar shapes,
accustomed shapes,
while in my palm, a pool of warm,
a failing breath of moon,
the broken columella of my heart,
and the blue waters of the Aegean,
receding, receding.

## My Grandmother's Toes

I remember the mud mostly,
at Southend on Sea,
the way it squelched grey between toes
that were startlingly pink. Thick mud like molasses,
cool slime.

I remember my Grandma in a deckchair,
bundled-up in her winter coat, straw hat
like a donkey's, with ears poking out at the sides.

*You all right, Nan?* I'd ask. *D' you need anything?*
and she'd shake her head, Parma violet chins wobbling;
*Ooh no, dear,* she'd say. *Don't you worry*
*about me. I'm fine.*
Always fine, my Grandma, at Southend on Sea,
as if the sandcastles were enough, and the voices,
and the way the mud squelched grey between toes
that were startlingly pink.

I remember her toes, the first time; the way she
peeled off her stockings, strip-teasing,
her calves the colour of sand,
then her toes; a grown-up's toes, attached to a grown-up's feet.
How far had they walked? For how long, to end up here,
at Southend on Sea, with mud squelching grey
in between?

Side by side, a merry-go-rounding seagull behind,
someone took a photo, and there we are,
heads back and laughing, our faces scrunched up at the sun,
twenty toes wriggling into the lens, wriggling.
It's the toes that you notice;
like we're walking toward you, always approaching.

Tiny footsteps patter.
*Look*, she says, pressing her feet down hard in the mud.
*Look how it squelches! Doesn't it feel good?* -
beginning to sink now, very softly, reaching out her hands.
I stretch hard across the years;
*You all right, Nan?* I ask. *D' you need anything?*
*Ooh no, dear*, she says. *Don't you worry
about me. I'm fine.*

## The Wrong End of the Sparkler

Basil Brush on bonfire night,
and everywhere the smell of woodsmoke warm
with bursts of colour, dark air mingling tiny flecks
of feather-textured grey.

My small breath makes a baby ghost.
My sparkler fizzes, glows, snakes a zigzag trail
of hot down soft onto the grass. Its thin stalk burns
breath-red then blinks to black.
I reach to pick it up,
but sudden laughter booms distraction; Basil's
foxy banter through the window.
My fingers grasp
the wrong end of the sparkler.

Always looking frontways since, attending
to the job in hand,
while just behind me, doors swing shut, and circles close
a whispered kiss that leaves me on the outside looking in.
Nothing harsh, dramatic; the ache of
invitations missed, of conversations wasted,
my busy fingers harvesting the rot of things I
thought were true, but turned out hollow
in the end and cool and undesired.

The tree outside my window's turning buttered toast.
Its leaves will drop a smoky snow tomorrow,
burn breath-red then quickly blink to black.
I'll bury my hands in the fire, let the flames
engulf me.
Shadrach, Meshach, Abednigo. An angel
in the flame, a reconstruction.
I will grow new hands, a new self, choose again.

## David and Bathsheba

*Thus, there were fourteen generations in all from Abraham to David,*
*fourteen from David to the exile to Babylon,*
*and fourteen from the exile to Christ.*

*Matthew 1; vs 17*

Maybe one day I'll repent it,
but not this day,
not while she slumbers in my arms,
hair spilling like water across the pillows,
the myrrh on her skin singing spice through my blood.
She is my temple, my psalm.
Nothing before her. Nothing beyond.

I was lost the first night I saw her,
kneeling at the courtyard pool, her skirts
gathered about her waist,
cypress oil threading gold across her breasts;
a web of want to hook the heart of a king.
She came when I summoned her.
She lay with me,
and the radiance that spilled into the space
between our bodies
dazzled into dust the yoke of our vacuous pasts;
her husband,
my wife. A simple task.
One with a knife in his back,
the other desert-exiled, disremembered.

Now, there is only this moon-shattered
night in which we meet,
this point of no return returned to us
hour by hour, wet with love;
ourselves constantly fragmenting, reassembling.
I may die of it, but I will not repent it,
and if my sins should one day be visited
on my sons, my grandsons, their sons...
If one among them should be made to pay
for the evil I have done in the name of love,
then so be it,
for we have tasted God on each other's lips,
Bathsheba and I, sharp as poison.
We arise each day from a sleep like death,
and drink again.

## Love in the Language of Horses

When you Connemara toward me across the dance floor,
your eyes Sable Island and full of Criollo,
I take your hand and we
Falabella back and forth,
our hearts insistent and burning with Mustang.
We Missouri Fox Trotter until the sun goes down;
your Haflingers light about my waist,
your Knabstrup like a secret breathed between us.
And then, soft as Shag-ia, you suggest,
Bardigiano
I say yes without thinking,
and we Palomino home as fast as our
Fredericksborgs will carry us.

Inside your room,
Galiceno with lamplight,
you Bashkir my Pottocks,
and Wurttemburg my Suffolk Punch,
until I....*Appaloosa*!, again and again,
paroxysms of New Forest Pony gripping my body,
and then,
as Kabardin as I can,
I Belgian Warmblood your Knabstrup until it
quivers with Caspian, and you Hackney Horse into my Karabakh.
Then we curl, Akhal-Teke and Fjord,
our limbs heavy with Gelderlander,
sleeping until Morgan moves at the window.

At breakfast, we Cleveland Bay,
a little Cheval De Merens in the Morgan light,
until, Lusitano, you take my Haflingers
in your own and Konik them as if they are Sorraia.
American Shetland suddenly and Shire,
I see you for the Thoroughbred you are, and know
that I would like you
to Wurttemburg my Suffolk Punch
until the Norman Cobs come Hucul.

# Falling in Love With the Lion

If I'd been there, in the den,
instead of Daniel,
I wouldn't have cared if King Darius and the others
had loitered on the balcony, watching.
I'd have done it anyway;
fallen in love with the lion.

When he came swaggering toward me,
blond-maned, his huge paws like
small continents, nudging at my knees,
I'd have leant in close and breathed
the heavy musk of his pelt,
touched my fingertips to the crisscross
sky of scars on his muzzle.
I'd have rested my head against
his neck, felt his sinew stretch
and bone dissolve to solve
the sudden mystery of a girl who didn't fear him.

He'd have spoken then,
his muzzle thrust forward,
eyes half-closed in concentration,
expelling every ounce of air from deep down
in his chest;
a sound
like thunder in the desert.

They'd have heard it miles away,
in Egypt, Samaria, south to the sea of Galilee,
where the warm air would have claimed it,
rained it
as an echo on the distant Masai Mara,
the blood-red place of his birth.
And a Martial Eagle, high on its rocky perch,
its spotted ermine feathers
fluttering in the breeze,
would have lifted its face to a fleet of flat-bottomed clouds
and replied;
*Simba kuonekana upendo kudumu;*
*The lion has found love at last.*

## The Blue Touch of Love

Away for the summer,
I gave you my plant
to look after. I knew
it would thrive with you;
sitting warmly
on your windowsill,
looking out over green
ground toward the cathedral,
or leaning in to catch
the murmur of your singing
voice about the flat.
My cold room would have
killed it, and because
we two had loved each other
softly for a while,
I felt that it would sense
a safety in your smile,
and be a leafy part
of me extended to your touch.

Returning in September,
I stumbled in to find
your new love stretched out
slimly, darkly on the rug;
flicking practiced fingers
through a glossy magazine.
You grimly shook your head.
*I watered it regularly,*
*put it in the sun, just*
*like you said, but...well...*
and there it sat, dead.

A sacrifice to strange things
mutely witnessed,
things which would have
withered my soul too,
but hurrying home, a mound
of brown decay,
I sensed a pale shoot
differently conceived,
struggling to the blue
touch of love.
Your dark girl smiling
on the rug; the flowers
she brought with her, all
in bloom.

## A Dream of Falling

They said he was drunk,
he and his friends stumbling
back to their camp-site,
somewhere in the pitch black
Devon night.

They said he ran ahead, laughing,
frightening the cows, until
he reached a tall fence
dividing the fields, or so
they thought. He didn't even
pause, but clambered over,
disappeared.

They heard his cries; sharp,
surprised and when they reached
the fence they found no other
field beyond - only
the cliff-edge, a sheer drop
into darkness.

Sometimes I wake from a dream
of falling; feel the cold
air rushing past my ears,
black skies swimming.
Sometimes I wake recalling
him, feeling his surprise,
hearing only the crash of waves
and cows lowing in the darkness.

## Walk With Me

I walk a tiled line between the beds,
aware of eyes that follow keenly
my sure steps, envious of my walking.
Old ladies now who sit propped up
without their teeth, whose longings
stroll with me the years to girlhood.

Arm-in-arm through meadow hush,
the green-gold of a thousand springs;
they stretch their limbs, they ride their
bikes, run smiles back and forth through
treasured nylons, and I pass by,
guilty of the youth I take for granted,
while legs, a dead-weight now beneath the covers,
stir but for a moment and are still.

## You

Before the dark bounced high
a moon to fill my view, before the circle closed to
now, and all of this, and you, I wonder, did we meet?
Nudge shoulders on a snaking street, apologise
and hurry on our way, or maybe glare an amber black,
and grumble as our bodies sparked apart.
When you were just a face, a set of limbs,
a rivulet of colour on the pavement, at the counter,
an unremarked on walker in the park.
Did I not see and *know* that it was you?

How is it that we sat that day, (if indeed there *was* a day)
with elbows touching
in the waiting room, and all I felt
was bone and brown, a blur of warm, a shape
that didn't fit inside its clothes.
How *could* I not have known that it was you?
No tiny beak to tap a signal deep inside the egg.
No message curling up like smoke to say
how easily our future could have changed its mind
and turned and walked away.

Now, my hands are cupped for every drop,
and love is like the sea that creeps to fill
my moat scored lightly in the sand. My castle
stands, while softly round it water
laps as green as all the days before you came.
Still, there is fear, and random stars
that blink and stare and keep their secrets
safe. Who else is there?

Outside I walk a careful line, my heart a searchlight
burning in the blue. I stop myself
from running up to strangers, peering closely,
asking very softly, *Is it you? Please, is it you?*

## Ratified
*For Gilbert*

Nothing's the same since you came;
my world is changed -
a second heartbeat in the night and little footsteps
light on the rungs of your ladder.
I hear you running through my dreams;
the breeze of my breath in your whiskers,
your long nose scenting the suburbs of rat heaven.

You run for miles every night,
so far away and out of sight
I sometimes think, that's it,
you're gone for good,
but then, waking;
the staccato click of tiny teeth
on sunflower seeds,
and I know you've made it home.

It's not as if I haven't shared my room
with rats before, but they were
altogether bigger.
Sometimes they stole the whole duvet away,
and mumbled in the dark about football.
Their body hair was coarse against my skin,
and they often *didn't* make it home by morning.

You are nicer to touch.
You smell better.
You are always pleased to see me,
and though your testicles are huge
and quite resplendent, you don't flaunt them,
don't have them on display.
Instead, you simply sit sideways
and look at me as if to say,
*What, **these** old things?*

If you were a man, you'd be
George Clooney,
but I'm glad you're not a man.

Come, take my hand,
show me the way to rat heaven.

## Diving For Pearls

My lover is diving for pearls,
his long body stretching through blue,
slipping in shadow; his changing feet
like tiny fins again. The startled fish
who swim this space, fan
troubled tails and, turning, race
to follow where he leads. Their black
mouths open wide, swallow the surprise
of a body in the water, a bronze boy
in the water. A downward blur of bubbles
make his mark, and small stones
shine like tiny moons against
his curve of dark.

I watch his fingers rippling.
I watch his body bloom; a small narcissus
breaking through an arc of ocean gloom.
He rolls pale worlds like vowels
upon his tongue, tasting beauty,
tasting things to come, and yet
his eyes are strangely sad in surfacing
with up-turned palms, with lost
and empty hands. He cannot meet my gaze.

He cannot bring me pearls to taste,
nor gold to wear, nor promises, nor praise.
Instead he brings me treasures
of a different kind; a voice
with which to sing. Heart of my heart.
Mind of my mind. Warm life, like water,
tumbles from his skin.
And always, he's the point
of my arriving. Unravelling the thread
of who I am, here I begin.

We sleep where sea spray touches
golden sand; together turned by gentle
tides, forgiven now, our bones
washed white - we leave ourselves
behind. And in the morning, when
they come, what will they find?
A brightness diffusing.
Two tongues of flame. Pearls and petals
falling from the sky like rain.

## Abishag

They have brought me to the bed of the old king,
to warm him, to lay my head
against his puckered breast and melt him back to life.
They have smeared my cheeks with galera,
my skin with myrrh.
They have taken away my clothes.

The icy vessel of his body must be my child now.
I must fold my fire around him,
press my palms to the clay of his thighs,
his chest, the grey cave of his belly.
I must remember that he is my king,
how once, when he was young, he threw off
his robes and danced all night before the Lord;
black hair flying, bare feet sounding
a rhythm of praise on the stone steps of the temple.

I must remember his glory,
but deep in the night, the moonlight
shows him to me; an old man,
his mouth fallen open, the white tips of his teeth
slick with saliva like the teeth of an animal,
and the petals of my sex close like a fist
and will not open.

Then, I long for the mountains of Shunem,
the olive groves, the blue waters of Beersheba.
I long for the boy who pressed
pomegranates to my lips, his eyes the colour of cedarwood,
his skin as smooth as fruit beneath my fingers,
and I close my eyes to the moonlight,
lean my ear to the fading beat
of the old man's life. It drips
like a tap in the darkness;
*Soon. Soon. Soon.*

## Sex Like Dancing

It *is*, if you think about it;
a kind of fandango with edges that you hadn't fathomed.
A way of knowing what God looks like.
He is Braille beneath your fingertips suddenly.
Can you feel him?
The small of a back,
the shape of a breast,
the way a chest
slopes, as fluid as the ocean you think you hear
when someone says your name in a voice that is not their own,
in a voice that you have given them, with your hands,
your tongue.

It's a miracle. An eccentric
flamenco.
Can you hear those castanets?
The rush-hush of skin on skin?
Maracas too, at the back of it all,
hard to know
who's inside who.

It's a party number.
A song sung in its composition.
Don't let anyone tell you different.
Take it into your mouth, dissolve it,
let the music convince you into a conga right around the block.
Lift your arms into the air and share
the bare-faced cheek
of how pleased you are to have discovered
this new skill, a hot-shoe shuffle,
a tango of toes intertwining,
a foxy trot between the sheets,
a live jive.

Sex like dancing.
Ah, but love, like that last tipsy sway to a tune you don't know,
empty bottles everywhere,
and the band getting ready to go home.

## Soap Suds

There was a time when all I knew
were soap suds in your sink,
the red of rugs, and mushrooms in a pan.
There was a time I'd stay where I'd been put,
short legs dangling, watching you wash up.
My mother's mouth would talk and you
would smile, answer back. There was a time
when that was all I knew. And then I grew
to knowing more.

Tuesday afternoons we'd step outside. We'd walk
what felt like far and there you'd be.
Soap suds, red rugs, mushrooms in a pan,
and in your hand, a glass of orange squash
for me. My mother's friend, like my friends,
only tall; your smile somehow too big for your face.
I'd drink my orange squash and watch,
and *that* was what I knew; to drink
it down and peer right through; see you inside out-
side nubbled glass,
orange gone but you made round behind my fuzzy
telescopic eye. Distorted, not quite who you were;
soap suds, red rugs, mushrooms, all askew,
and you.

Grown up a long time now, I watch
but you don't see, don't circle soft with smiles,
orange squash, don't even really quite remember me,
although you try, your mouth tries out
the shadow of my name. But time has sunk things deep;
the self who knew, the heart that juggled choices
in what seems a dream, but once was
just a yes where someone lived.
Soap suds, red rugs, mushrooms in a pan.
*That* is what we knew. You knew it too,
but now the empty glass is in *your* hand,
held to *your* eyes; a telescopic lens
that lies, and though I surface from the soapy blue,
you only stare, stare hard, stare through,
see out the other side to where our Tuesdays were,
but they aren't there for you.
Nothing looks the same behind
your eyes, and I'm just someone that they say you knew.

## Somewhere Over Gelsenkirchen

Somewhere over Gelsenkirchen
you came down, trailed a yearning
greyly through the cloud
and fell to earth.
Perhaps you have a grave somewhere.
Perhaps somewhere there's substance
then to something I have only
known as shadow.

An uncle on whose knee I never
sat, who never married, lost
his hair; grew old or fat.
Perhaps it's strange that all
the uncles I *have* known,
who've pinched my cheek and made
me dance at weddings, have seemed
lacking. Less a presence than
the face that smiles from
your picture; neat in your uniform,
your cap worn at a jaunty angle.

You were a navigator; pencilling
a route to outwit death,
but he disguised himself that night;
wore the mantle of a purple
dusk and lay in wait.
I'm the same age now as you were
then, and though I often think
I hear the hum of engines
in the sky, I know that you're
elsewhere.

Can't you navigate a route to me;
give substance to the shadow
of your smile?
Or are you still trying to outwit
the dusk, somewhere
over Gelsenkirchen?

# Making a Difference

You tell me they have been a waste,
these years I have spent
ensnared by books; counter-bound
and stamping Barbara Cartlands.
You say there are a thousand
more worthwhile things I could
have done, being young, instead
of this prosaic job revered
by none. Perhaps you're right.

I could have packed a rucksack,
travelled widely, helped aid some
lost and dying mountain tribe,
or turned my thoughts to stage school,
worn black leggings, appeared
at Stratford with the RSC.
I could have juggled figures at a big
desk, played with stocks and shares,
made lots of cash, or maybe studied
medicine at Cambridge, pioneered
cures, healed the sick.

There are indeed a thousand
things I could have done, being young,
but I have measured time here
in little triumphs; smiles,
gestures, words which have to some
degree at least, helped ease the load.
I haven't tried to save the world.
My name won't be remembered.
Big issues I have left to someone
else. Instead, I've helped old ladies
find their favourite books,
have asked about their children,
their arthritis; have laughed
with them at dreary English weather,
and if they've smiled, or gripped
my hand, or said, *God bless you, dear,*
I know I've made a difference,
a very tiny difference, and isn't
that what matters? Isn't it
such that we are here?

## Hurrying Nun

*After the Painting 'New York Pavements' by Edward Hopper*

Where is she going,
that nun with the baby carriage?
Where is she going? Her black back catches
a glare of sunlight, returns it without telling
where it is she is going,
but her cheeks are pink from hurrying,
pink as the puff of blanket which covers the baby
asleep in the baby carriage.
A hot day, New York windows opening
to a trickle of breeze, but the nun doesn't notice the heat.
The streets are white beneath the wheels of the baby carriage,
white as the face of God beneath her hurrying feet.

Where is she going?
How long has she been missing from the cool corridors
of the convent?
Perhaps she only meant to step outside into the sunshine,
walk a little way, feel what the day was like,
but then...
the baby carriage, safe with its brake on outside the baker's window.
She would have looked inside;
swaddling clothes, sweet smell of straw,
a Christ-child asleep beneath the black-framed star of her face,
and suddenly, the sunlight would no longer
have been enough, nor the wavering sky, bright blue
with the breath of her God.
Nothing would have been enough,
but the baby in the baby carriage.

Now, she knows where she is going.
Back down the hot streets of Summer,
her small feet are running,
blank body racing to catch the curl of a blossom which falls
from the branch of a tree she remembers.
She must catch it before it touches the pavement,
wear it like the mark of Cain.
Crooning hallelujahs, she must open
her mouth to the sweet tongue of sin,
shuffle off her skin
and slip into the future with the baby in the baby carriage.

# Magdalen

If they try to tell you that it wasn't love,
don't believe them.
How could they know what it was,
when all they did that day was stand and watch;
faces growing cloudy with doubt,
fingers hot as candlewax
clutching empty cups, while the wine soured.

They didn't feel the measure of it stir inside my chest.
They wouldn't even come near me,
but *he* came,
covered my cheeks with the palms of his hands,
slipped off his heavy robes to kneel before me on the cold stone floor
and look
until my body turned itself to light and water.

He smelt of cypress wood. He smelt of the road;
his clothes filled with travel and the brawl of foreign tongues.
I bathed his feet with the scent of my tears,
touched my lips to the dust
that lived
in the veins of his ankles.
I dried his feet with the falling-black bloom of my hair,
and covered my face that no-one might know me,
but *he* knew me.
He knew the curse of my name long before
their black mouths spat it out,
but he anointed it, made it mean a different thing;
*she who is forgiven.*

If they try to tell you that it wasn't love,
don't believe them,
for I have heard my name playing like music
on the lips of my God, and now, I follow him;
Capernaum, Jerusalem,
Gethsemane, Golgotha.

He will have need of me.
When they slip off his heavy robes and lay him
before me on the cold stone floor,
I will bathe his ruined feet with the scent
of my tears again, and press his crushed palms to the swell
of my belly.
The heartbeat there grows stronger every day.

## The Story Cheetahs

They would come to her at night,
the story cheetahs,
stalking over pavements to her window,
climbing the shadows to sink down beside her as she slept;
their long whiskers tickling her cheeks,
warm breath smoky with the scents of the Masai Mara.

A child back then, I heard her name them,
heard the words that meant they kept her snug as love on a Winter's night,
and I pictured them,
stretched across the bed, curling their bodies
delicately around her, while her fingers
traced the shape of flight beneath pale swirls of fur.

I listened for their stories;
heard the purr
of Africa -
And I longed for the story cheetahs to come to me.

Only later, lifting myself clear of the colours of childhood,
I asked; How had she summoned them?
What had made them come?
And she laughed at me, said the words slowly;
*storage heaters,* started talking about
utility bills and economy seven heating,
and my heart buckled hard into a fist that really hasn't
opened since,
but I know it would, even now,
if they came.

Nightly, I listen for the sound of footsteps,
a low growl of welcome,
their small faces, tear-stained black at my window ledge.
I still believe they'll come.
How could they not,
when the shining grass of the Mara awaits me,
and the last hour of daylight,
and the quicksilver heels of delusion.

# Following the Owl

It wasn't even dark, not very late,
when a moving bruise of blue against
the grey, caught us, halted, ankle-deep in words.
One finger to your lips you turned
and ran, called for me to follow;
springing soft across the forest floor,
pointing held-in whistling breath
toward a quickly fading smudge of dusk.

And I followed though the trees grew
strangely restless, their fingers closing tight
across the sky. I followed though
their faces yawned and voices hooted,
*Oh, how slow! Your earth-bound*
*feet will never catch what flies!*
And even when the bracken cracked,
and jagged bone sprang from the black,
I tried to run and tried to reach
the filaments of shadow,
tried to want that shining thing,
tried hard to match my own desire to yours.

But somewhere in the breathing dusk,
I caught another's voice, looked up
to see two eyes, two blades of bright,
felt the silk and sinew stretch, felt
a fur-warmth circling breath -
the last of hope, the leafy touch of death.

I saw us from the branches, love;
two dormice scuttling hard toward the light,
our fumbling feet, our tiny dreams,
stalked down, devoured in the owl-cold night.

## I've Always Wanted a Cowboy

I've always wanted a cowboy,
with a thick moustache and buckskin gloves.
Along he'd come on his feisty mustang,
just as the sun was setting,
just in time,
and he'd scoop me up like a bundle of clothes from the road.

I'd be startled at first, but I'd cover it well,
wouldn't wince at the bitter coffee he offered
when we stopped to camp for the night,
wouldn't balk at the howling of wolves,
and when he peeled off his shirt to shake out the dust,
I wouldn't snigger at his high-buttoned long johns.
He'd spread out a blanket, build a small fire,
kick off his stovepipe boots.

High above us, in a curve of prairie dark,
a sliver of moon would flirt with the stars,
and the cowboy would lay aside
his Colt 45 to croon me a song.
His voice would be apple-wood sweet,
warm with the afterglow of a day on the road.

Nearby, his horse would snuffle in the moonlight,
nibbling at the grass, and the cowboy would
lower his Stetson to turn the world dark.
*Tomorrow'll be a long day, per'ty lady*, he'd say. *Best rest up.*
But I wouldn't.
Instead, I'd snake myself close like an Indian brave,
summon the cunning of the entire Sioux nation to teach my fingers
a way inside
those high-buttoned long johns.
I'd take my cowboy by surprise.

## Levi

Look out for him Dad, because he'll be small
and I've always thought of where you are
as being big.
Are there trees there? He'd like it if there were.
He was always a good climber.
Remember that Christmas when he was a kitten
and he clambered up the curtains
and made Mum swear?
She didn't like him very much back then,
but today she said she'll miss him.
Today she said her world won't be the same
now that he's gone.

I was still at school when he arrived;
thirteen, dipping my toes into the waters
of a grown-up world and not liking the feel.
You bought me a cat to compensate,
but the lady in the pet shop said he was
the runt of the litter; thin, even for a Siamese -
tail too short, eyes not blue enough,
but the way he curled his body like a comma
to accommodate our touch.
We loved him almost at once.

All that Winter you were ill, he sat on your lap, remember?
He kept away the chill and looked into your face
as if he knew.
He searched for you for ages when you left,
sat in your chair with his back straight, waiting.
We've been doing the same today,
expecting him home; a little Lazarus, unsteady on his feet,
blinking into sunlight.

People will say we're making a fuss.
They'll say, he was only a cat,
and they'll be right, of course, but what I remember most,
is that he is who I loved the very first time that I loved,
at thirteen, uncovering a seam
of gold beneath the surface. He gave the word its weight,
and proved that thing they say about how God
can come in small shapes too.

So, please look out for him Dad.
I know that he'll be looking out for you.

## Poppies

When my old lover calls, I remember the poppies.
His voice is scarlet with them, heavy
with the blood-rush red of kneeling in the grass before
the rains came on.
We gathered them fast, a harvest of poppies,
breathing them in all the way to the lake
where their flame
was a flag and our fingertips
played on the petals as if they were strings.
I remember the silk and the pollen-haze puff
from their mouths, and the moonlight that
rippled toward us a column of yellow; toward us,
away from us, into each other.

When my old lover calls, I remember the poppies,
wanting to carry them home, wanting their crimson tide
to tumble moonlight through my rooms, splash
shrieks of colour at my shuttered windows,
but when we came to pick them up, they crumpled into
nothing in our fingers, broke apart like promises
and fell a long way down into the dark.

When my old lover calls, he asks;
*Do you remember the poppies?*
I tell him no. I tell him I don't like poppies.
I tell him they're a waste of time because they never last.
These days, I say, my favourite things are
pot plants that endure,
but when my old lover calls, deep down, I
remember the poppies, and long for the poppies;
opening my mouth to the pollen-haze puff
of their breath, drinking them in for the hour
they have, for the ruby-fine
silk of their coming, a mingling of moonlight.
Deep down, I remember the poppies.
Deep down, where my old lover calls,
my body's ablaze with the poppies.

## Pheasant

Skies as blue as true love and a breeze in the trees.
We cruise the countryside.
One hand on the steering wheel, the other resting quietly on your thigh,
I feel the ache of doubting break, and try
to melt my self-imposed denials down to dust.

My eyes veer always from the winding road to look at you.
Green fields, grey heedless sheep flick quickly by
while I look long at you; your hands, a small cathedral curled;
dark eyes shy and startled, sad, sardonic all at once.
I watch the changing seasons of your face;
try to live my moment in a space of sunlight, certainty and grace.
I wait the signals of your changing face.
And the bird of all my loving settles softly in your lap,
sings you a smile.
I, smiling too, turn back toward the road ahead,
too late to see, yet seeing sudden green-gold-red;
a flash of pheasant lost beneath my wheels. The little thud that sickens,
and in the rear view mirror, a blur of blood and feathers.

Tears in my eyes, I turn to you,
wanting words to make the sadness better.
You shrug and pat my leg;
*Pheasants are stupid, always getting run over.*
And we drive a while in silence. My eyes on the road.
Your hand on my leg. At the corners of my vision,
I can see that you are grinning. A chuckle in your voice, you say;
*Each time you change gear, I feel the muscles*
*tighten right up here in your thigh.*
A time ago, this would have made me glad, but now the focus alters.
Now, I'm thinking of the pheasant; wondering,
remembering what other things have fallen while I've had my eyes on you,
what other beauties I've ignored; what other loves I've trampled.
For often, I have seen a sudden green-gold-red;
a flash of something lost before I managed to distinguish
what it was. Too busy looking at you.
Too busy trying to make you look at me.

Now, you fiddle with the radio, and hum along to The Carpenters;
your fingers bouncing smugly on my thigh.
Some way behind us, the bird of all my loving blurs.

## The Wedding at Cana

I didn't even notice him at first;
just a face in the crowd, a wedding guest like me,
dusty with travel,
bewildered by the brawl of foreign tongues.
He was a stranger at the table, his face turned vaguely away from me,
nothing to hint at the fact that there would be
a miracle in his keeping.

The wedding blankets were spread like leaves,
drums and flutes like laughter.
The happy couple danced. We drank the wine;
a crimson glimmer in our mouths,
until the jars ran dry.
And it was then, that he turned to me,
the man I'd barely noticed, the stranger at the table.
His eyes as blue as the waters of Beersheba, he turned to me,
moving his hands over the stone jars as if they were alive;
surmising, transforming.
He turned the water into wine.
The man I'd barely noticed.
The one *least* likely.

But that's what it's like sometimes;
the one you barely notice, who slips by you on the street,
sits alongside you at the wedding table,
lives in the house next to yours -
the one least likely,
because suddenly, they'll turn to look at you
and a miracle will lift and fall.
Blue as the waters of Beersheba,
your world will shine.
It's the alchemy of the unexpected;
lead into gold, friendship into love, water into wine.

# Spitfire

*My* father was there when it happened.
He even saw the pilot's face;
tired, day-old stubble, the silver glint
of a chain on the lapel of his flying jacket.

They'd been struggling with arithmetic all morning,
but the staccato tap of chalk on the blackboard couldn't
distract them from the Spitfires taking off and landing
beyond the perimeter fence.
The school trustees hadn't
bargained on the Battle of Britain happening in term-time.
Now, all the boys in the top floor rooms
had panoramic views of the airfield.
Arithmetic didn't stand a chance.

But my *father* was there when it happened.
Just before the lunchtime bell,
a sound like a car backfiring.
Early spring, and the sky was egg-shell blue;
a Spitfire climbing away, nothing unusual,
but the drumbeat of its engine failing, resuming,
failing.
Perhaps the pilot meant to pass overhead,
land safe on the unpeopled fields which stretched in the distance,
but all those faces at the window! What if his engine
gave out altogether? What if he dropped like a rock
through the roof of the classroom?

My father was *there* when it happened,
when the pilot changed direction, veered away from the school,
deliberately ploughed the nose of the plane down into
the empty playing fields.

Much later, my father, tucked up like a child
in the last of his hospital beds,
the drumbeat of his breathing failing, resuming,
failing.
He feels for my hand, whispers; *Go now. Don't need to stay,* -
wants to spare me,
but I do not want to be spared.
I want to keep him talking, keep him airborne,
to see his face turned toward me and *know* that it's still him.
I want to stay until it's over, so that later I can say
my father *was* there when it happened.

## David

The other day, on a bus, in the rain,
I thought of your name, David,
and the sun came out in my heart
and stayed all day.
This was always your way, your gift -
to lift us,
coax us into smiling with your smile,
shape us into shining as you shone;
that never-fading twinkle in your eye,
your sense of humour,
sense of beauty,
sense of fun.
You saw us at our best,
and at our worst,
and loved us anyway,
trying to convey that every day
was something to be cherished.
You were right.

When we were children, you and I,
I fell into a river;
you gave me your clothes to wear.
I tumbled over the handlebars of my bike;
you carried me all the way home.
I got stung by a bee;
you slipped your arm around me and said
it should have been *you* stung instead.
The boy I knew,
the man *we* knew -
the two aren't far removed.

David, for the time that you were with us
we are grateful,
for the days to come without you,
we will grieve,
but the legacy you leave us
is that anywhere and everywhere,
all we ever need to do
is think of you, think of your name,
and the sun will come out in our hearts
and stay all day.

## Keeper of the Flame

The keeper of the flame came again
today, nodding his head,
full of air and whispers, saying;
*You. Me. Old friends.*
He'd have me believe love is all,
a living sacrifice, a shape to climb into,
sleep tight.
He'd have me double back and do it all again,
I know he would, and
not reluctantly either, but waving
my arms in the air like a charismatic Christian,
jubilant at the boot in the face,
a graceless heap shrugged off and left
for dead.
The keeper of the flame gets his kicks
like this, setting a puzzle to which there
is no answer. Bastard.
Next time he comes, tap-tapping at the glass
with his; *You. Me. Old friends.*
I'll invite him in with a banana grin,
and blow out his flame with a breath;
birthday candle, puff of smoke.
*You. Me. Old friends.*
Bollocks.

## Prince and Lady Prolonging Intercourse With a Cup of Tea

*After an eighteenth century Indian illustration.*

But it wouldn't, would it?
All that hot water swilling about,
and where would they balance the pot?
Picking tea leaves out of your teeth
is hardly a turn-on,
and what if one of them wanted Canderel
and the other didn't?
Only good thing,
there'd always be somewhere to hang the cosy.